ALL ABOUT THE RODEO

RODEO STEER WRESTLERS

Lynn Stone

Rourke

Publishing LLC
Vero Beach, Florida 32964

www.rourkepublishing.com

Photo credits:
Front cover ribbon and background illustration © Shanna M Korby, front cover photo © Jim Parkin, back cover © Olivier Le Queinec, all other photos © Tony Bruguiere except page 5 © 4loops, page 17 © Jim Parkin, page 21 © Travis black, page 29 © Tom Marvin

Editor: Jeanne Sturm

Cover and page design by Nicola Stratford, Blue Door Publishing

Library of Congress Cataloging-in-Publication Data

Stone, Lynn M.
  Rodeo steer wrestlers / Lynn M. Stone.
      p. cm. -- (All about the rodeo)
  Includes index.
  ISBN 978-1-60472-391-5
  1. Steer wrestling--Juvenile literature. 2. Steer roping--Juvenile
literature. I. Title.
  GV1834.45.S73S86 2009
  791.8'4--dc22
                              2008018796

Printed in the USA

CG/CG

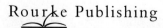

Rourke Publishing

www.rourkepublishing.com – rourke@rourkepublishing.com
Post Office Box 3328, Vero Beach, FL 32964

Table Of Contents

Steer Wrestling

The idea of locking horns, so to speak, with a steer is not most people's idea of a good time. After all, it's dirty and dangerous. For steer wrestlers, however, riding a sprinting horse to catch a running steer and bring it to a quick stop is pure delight.

Steer in his grasp, a steer wrestler's boots become his brakes.

Steer wrestling, also known as **bulldogging**, is one of the seven standard events at most major rodeos. Along with team roping, tie-down roping, and barrel racing, steer wrestling is one of the timed events. In steer wrestling, a cowboy's style, or lack of it, doesn't count for or against him. It's the time that counts.

The cowboy, his horse, and the steer are the major players in rodeo steer-wrestling events.

A cowboy swings in one motion from horseflesh to cowflesh.

But the event could not unfold without another horse and rider, the **hazer**, in the **arena**. The hazer's job is to, well, steer the steer.

Hazer (left) helps keep the steer running close to the bulldogger's horse.

The start of a steer wrestling performance is no time to leave your seat, or even blink! Steer wrestlers, hazers, and their horses work so skillfully together that each steer-wrestling run is normally completed in just five to six seconds. The world record is an amazing 2.4 seconds. Can you think of a faster event in any sport?

Down and dirty, a bulldogger flips the steer onto its back.

A cowboy plows the arena dirt in bringing a steer's run to a sharp stop.

⭐ Unlike some rodeo events, steer wrestling did not
⭐ **evolve** from real cowboy chores, such as roping or
⭐ **breaking** horses to a saddle. Cowboys had no reason to
⭐ do something as foolhardy as leaping onto a 600-pound
⭐ (273-kilogram) package of horn and muscle. Instead,
⭐ steer wrestling evolved from the amazing imagination of
⭐ one man, William (Bill) Pickett.

Running the Event

Like other rodeo events, steer wrestling takes place in an arena, indoors or outdoors, day or night, but always on a dirt floor.

A steer-wrestling contest begins with a steer placed in a **chute** at one end of the arena. The chute is flanked by two holding areas called boxes. The contestant and his horse are in the box to the left of the steer chute. The hazer waits atop his horse in the box to the steer's right. Both horsemen wait behind a rope barrier.

Ranch cowboys had enough hard work without wrestling steers for sport.

Teamwork is essential after the steer is released into the arena.

The steer is released first, giving it a brief head start. As the steer bolts from the chute, it trips the barrier rope of the horse boxes. The steer wrestler charges toward the left side of the steer. The hazer rides to the steer's right. The two horses keep the steer loosely sandwiched and running in a straight line.

The steer is barely out of the chute before being bulldogged.

It's a brief run. Accelerating to nearly 30 miles per hour (48 kilometers per hour), the cowboy's horse quickly overtakes the steer, perhaps now 150 feet (46 meters) and four seconds from the starting gate. The steer wrestler leans off the right side of his horse, shifts his weight from horse to steer, and reaches for the steer's head with both hands. The cowboy leaves the saddle as his horse dashes ahead and away from the steer.

Coordination and timing are critical as a cowboy slides from horse to steer.

The cowboy grabs the steer's left horn in his left hand. He corrals the steer's right horn in the crook of his right arm, gaining an ironlike grip on the animal's head. With his boots extended forward, the steer wrestler's feet hit the ground, skidding and plowing up the arena dirt.

At this point, as the cowboy forcefully plants his feet, he uses his grip and strength to force the steer over and onto the ground. The cowboy's timing here is critical, because he also uses the steer's forward **momentum** to help throw the animal off balance. The steer must still be standing when the cowboy begins to throw it.

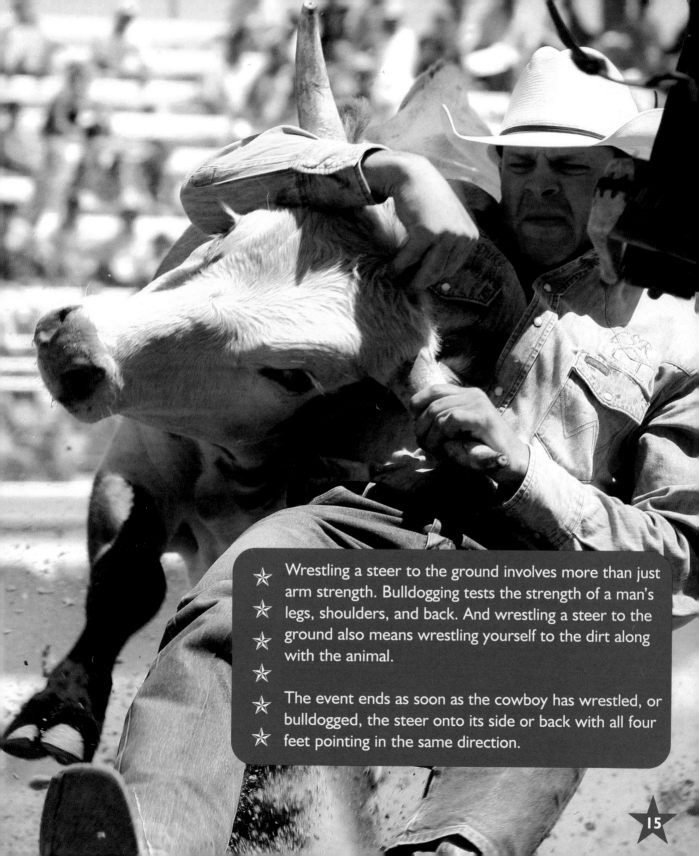

Wrestling a steer to the ground involves more than just arm strength. Bulldogging tests the strength of a man's legs, shoulders, and back. And wrestling a steer to the ground also means wrestling yourself to the dirt along with the animal.

The event ends as soon as the cowboy has wrestled, or bulldogged, the steer onto its side or back with all four feet pointing in the same direction.

15

The Riders

Steer wrestling is often called a big man's event. That is entirely reasonable, because a steer wrestler must stop, then knock over, a horned animal that outweighs him by 200 pounds (91 kilograms) or more. Strength is essential for a steer wrestler. However, there is more to the sport than brute force. A steer wrestler's **technique** in grasping the steer and applying the right amount of leverage to knock the animal over is also important.

> ★ One of the most talented bulldoggers in recent years has been Trevor Brazile. Born in 1976, Brazile is the first cowboy to qualify in four Professional Rodeo Cowboys Association (PRCA) National Finals Rodeo events, including steer wrestling.

The Horses and Steers

The bulls ridden in rodeos come from a variety of cattle **breeds** and mixes of breeds. The cattle in the steer-wrestling event, though, are usually of the Corriente breed.

Bulldogging favors tough, wiry Corriente steers.

This is fitting, because, like cowboy skills, Corriente cattle date back many generations in North America. The early Spanish explorers and conquistadores (conquerors) brought small, wiry cattle to the Americas from Spain in the late 15th century. They became the standard cattle of old Mexico and much of the Southwest before new beef breeds were introduced by American ranchers in the 1800s.

The fairly straight, medium length Corriente horns make the breed popular for bulldogging and roping events.

Newer, more modern breeds eventually displaced most of the Corrientes, but a few herds survived in the hands of cattle **fanciers**. Modern Corrientes still look much like their ancestors.

Corrientes are raised at this Florida ranch largely for rodeo events.

★ Corrientes are prized by steer wrestlers because their horns are an ideal length for grasping.

★ Corriente rodeo steers generally weigh from 400 to 600 pounds (182 to 273 kilograms).

21

A steer wrestler's horse is a highly trained athlete. The horse must be exceptionally quick for a short distance, and trusting of its rider. The best steer wrestling **mounts** are worth in excess of $30,000.

Forefeet in protective wrap, a bulldogger's horse dashes away from its rider.

Most steer wrestling mounts are quarter horses, the favorite horse of many working ranches as well as rodeos. Quarter horses are typically quick, strong, and compact. They do not have the long distance speed of **thoroughbreds**, nor do they need it. Quarter horses are rugged, and they can start and stop quickly.

Like their riders, rodeo quarter horses are superb athletes.

The History of Steer Wrestling

Bill Pickett is the father of steer wrestling. He was the only person to have single-handedly started a major rodeo event. Although steer wrestling has been generally for big men, Pickett, ironically, weighed about 145 pounds (66 kilograms). That did not prevent him from wrestling steers, and he did so in a most creative way.

Born in Texas, probably in 1870 or 1871, Pickett was of African American and American Indian descent. He and a brother started a horse breaking business, and Bill became a skilled rider. He later became a rodeo star and the first black cowboy actor, starring in *The Crimson Skull* and *The Bulldogger* in 1921.

Modern bulldoggers have followed in Bill Pickett's tradition.

No one knows for sure how Pickett started bulldogging. One story is that he simply lost his patience with an ill-tempered longhorn steer one day in 1903. According to that story, an angry Pickett leaped from his horse onto the longhorn and grabbed its horns. Pickett was not able to subdue the longhorn until he bit the steer's lower lip.

A fellow rodeo star of Pickett's, Matt Hinkle, told author Dora Scarbrough a somewhat different but similar story. Hinckle said that Pickett reacted angrily to a cow that had tried to **gore** his horse, Chico.

Pickett leaped onto the cow, grabbed her horns, and bit her lip. The cow went down, the story goes, but Pickett was afraid to release his lip lock for fear of being gored. Pickett escaped his dilemma with help from the ranch boss. How Pickett really discovered his talent will remain a mystery, since one of Pickett's brothers told yet a third version of how Bill began bulldogging.

The entire nation read about the lip biting bulldogger when Pickett wrestled a steer at the 1904 Cheyenne Frontier Days Rodeo. He eventually toured with the 101 Wild West Show. Pickett's fame grew, and bulldogging caught the attention of other cowboys. Pickett, however, remained the foremost bulldogger of his **era**.

Wild west show, 1933

Pickett was the first African American man elected to the National Cowboy Hall of Fame and Western Heritage Center. He was also **inducted** into the Rodeo Cowboy Hall of Fame. The Bill Pickett Invitational Rodeo celebrates his fame, and in 1993 the United States Postal Service issued a stamp in his honor.

In April 1932 Pickett died when a horse he was trying to rope kicked him in the head. Modern steer wrestlers owe Pickett a debt for beginning their sport, if not for making the lip biting of steers part of the process. Fortunately for modern bulldoggers, lip biting is neither required nor lawful.

A bulldogger downs a steer – without having to bite its lip!

Glossary

arena (uh-REE-nuh): the large enclosure in which rodeo and other events are held for public view

breaking (BRAYK-ing): the process of teaching a horse to accept a saddle and rider

breeds (BREEDZ): particular kinds of domestic animals within larger, closely related groups, such as the Corriente within the cattle group

bulldogging (BUL-dawg-ing): the act of wrestling a steer to the ground by grasping its head and neck; steer wrestling

chute (SHOOT): a tight, high-sided place in which individual animals can be contained and kept apart from each other

era (IHR-uh): a period of time marked by certain related events

evolve (i-VOLV): to gradually change

fanciers (FAN-see-urz): those who keep and have an affection for a certain kind of animal

gore (GOR): to injure with a sharp object, especially with an animal's horn

hazer (HAYZ-ur): a mounted cowboy whose job is to keep a steer running in a straight line during rodeo steer-wrestling competition

inducted (in-DUHK-tid): to have been officially brought into an organization as a part of it

momentum (moh-MEN-tuhm): energy to move forward

mounts (MOUNTS): animals upon which someone sits to ride, typically a horse

technique (tek-NEEK): a particular way of doing something

thoroughbreds (THUR-oh-breds): the foremost breed of racing horses

Further Reading

Want to learn more about rodeos? The following books and websites are a great place to start!

Books

Landau, Elle. *Bill Pickett: Wild West Cowboy.* Enslow, 2004.

Pinkney, Andrea. *Bill Pickett: Rodeo Ridin' Cowboy.* Harcourt Children's Books, 1999.

Sherman, Josepha. *Steer Wrestling and Roping.* Heinemann, 2001.

Websites

www.nlbra.com
www.longhornrodeo.com
www.prorodeo.org

Index

About The Author

Lynn M. Stone is a widely published wildlife and domestic animal photographer and the author of more than 500 children's books. His book *Box Turtles* was chosen as Outstanding Science Trade Book and Selectors' Choice for 2008 by the Science Committee of the National Science Teachers' Association and the Children's Book Council.